A Handbook For Adjunct/ Part-Time Faculty and Teachers of Adults

Revised Edition

Donald Greive, Ed.D.

INFO-TEC, Inc. • Cleveland, Ohio

To Order:

INFO-TEC, Inc.
P.O. Box 40092
Cleveland, Ohio 44140
(216) 333-3155

Fifth Printing, December 1992

Library of Congress
Catalog Card Number 90-083176
ISBN 0-940017-38-5 (P)
ISBN 0-940017-37-7 (C)

Printed in the United States of America

PREFACE

Increasing numbers of adult students in all types of educational institutions are being taught by part-time faculty. Thus, the role of part-time faculty will take on increasing importance in the decade ahead. Their continuing in-service development is an integral part of the success of the educational mission. Often, due to other career responsibilities, the part-time faculty member does not have the time or resources to adequately develop techniques and strategies necessary for a successful and satisfying teaching experience.

This publication is intended to help remedy that situation. *A Handbook for Adjunct/Part-Time Faculty and Teachers of Adults* is written at the practitioner's level emphasizing techniques and strategies of value to adjunct faculty. Although this publication is protected by copyright, it is the intent of the author that faculty receive the greatest support possible from its contents. Therefore, faculty are granted permission to reproduce for personal use any of the forms herein that have direct application to their teaching endeavors.

Donald Greive, Ed.D.

CONTENTS

ABOUT THE AUTHOR

Donald Greive is a former Dean of Academic, Evening, and Part-time Services at a Community College. He has served as a supervisor of student teachers at a state university and has been an adjunct faculty member at a liberal arts college, state university, community college, and technical institute.

He has been involved in adjunct faculty development and administration for many years and has served as a consultant in those areas. He has authored several articles and books addressing adjunct faculty, their needs, and related institutional concerns. He has managed national conferences on the topic of adjunct faculty development and management. He is presently the President of Info-Tec, Inc. providing consulting services to colleges and universities.

A Handbook
For Adjunct/
Part-Time
Faculty and
Teachers
of Adults

1

Teaching:
What It's All About

Orientation to College and Adult Teaching

During the decade of the 90's, teachers of college and adult students will be faced with many challenges that did not previously exist. Compared to the classroom of 25 years ago, the evolution is nearly complete to the modern classroom of the 21st century. The influx of a multi-cultural and multi-lingual student body, as well as the impact of technology, has caught the attention of educators everywhere. Not only is there cultural change in many of our classrooms through immigration and the raising of aspirations of many of our own citizens, the changing economic and political pressures throughout the world will impact education and thus its instructors.

As a teacher of the 1990's, you must be well-prepared for and open to the acceptance of these many changes. Whether you are working in a liberal arts college with tradition, values, campus ministry, and spiritual as well as intellectual development as the philosophy, in a community college where the role is to serve as an open door institution for opportunity (while at the same time providing technical skills and college transfer including associate degrees), a public university with its research and graduate emphasis, as well as undergraduate professional training, or an adult education center, you will feel the impact. The students of the 90's will be more highly motivated, more challenging and more enjoyable to teach.

With the concern for accountability and the realization that there are strategies and techniques to assist instructors, there is greater emphasis on improved teaching. The rise of the project technique in business and industry has probably provided impetus for its adoption by the educational community. Adult students of the 90's, employed in business and industry, will expect a planned and organized classroom. It is no longer a question whether there are going to be instructional objectives and strategies for teaching. It is a question of how skilled instructors are in developing and delivering them.

Already we are seeing signs of classrooms being fully equipped with computers. Projection devices are not uncommon. Many institutions have overhead projectors in every classroom. Video tape and television are common and rarely do we see the movie projector rolled in at specific times. Not only will faculty of the 90's need to understand this transition and cope with it, but often they will be required to utilize the technology as another activity in the motivation of students.

These factors, however, do not minimize the human element involved in being an instructor in the 90's. If you enjoy being a teacher, there is nothing wrong with telling the students that you are there because you enjoy teaching. Being cheerful, open, and understanding is always an asset to good teaching. Students in the 90's will like to hear your experiential anecdotes. Look upon the class as a project. Plan for it, motivate students, achieve objectives. Adult students expect planning and preparation and will not rebel if it is required. Expand your horizons. Be aware of your cultural and intellectual environment. Strive to be a good and successful instructor and your teaching experiences in the 90's will be exciting, rewarding, and satisfying.

It might be good for you to take a few moments before your first class to meditate about your purpose for teaching. This will do two things: it will encourage you to more clearly identify your role and personal goals and objectives, and it will increase your confidence. There may be students who question why someone of your caliber and expertise would spend their time in this endeavor. Be prepared. Have a few answers ready if students ask. If they don't ask, you might want to include it as a part of your introduction. You certainly have good reasons. It might be to your advantage to communicate them. The facts that you just enjoy teaching, like interaction with others, like the stimulation, enjoy being in front of a group, feel it improves your skills, and many other reasons you might identify are appropriate.

A commonly accepted axiom in education is that learning is best accomplished when there is a need for the learning and when it is built upon former learning and knowledge. From these observations we can conclude that most learning, contrary to popular belief, is not the responsibility of teachers. It is the responsibility of learners. Faculty, as facilitators, however, can utilize the above principles to ease the learning tasks of students. The ideal situation, of course, is one in which both the need and former knowledge are in proper perspective.

Learning starts with the knowledge and skills that students bring with them to class and not necessarily the content knowledge brought by faculty. Teaching is still a vocation, a calling, if you will, to individuals who enjoy being with people and feel intrinsic satisfaction in helping others and themselves to grow.

Characteristics of Good Teaching

Using one's mind in the pursuit of knowledge and at the same time sharing it with fellow citizens is in itself gratifying. The responsibility for a class and potential influence upon students are very stimulating. It remains stimulating, however, only so long as the instructor continues to grow and remain dynamic. The qualities of good teaching are quite simple:

- *Knowing your subject content.*
- *Knowing and liking students.*
- *Understanding our culture.*
- *Possessing command of professional teaching skills and strategies.*

Knowing your subject content means simply that you have a command of the expected knowledge of your discipline and the capability of calling upon resources. Knowing students is part of the teaching process and will be assisted with formal and informal communication within and outside the classroom. Understanding our culture has become more complex for the instructor of the 90's. Sensitivity to the diverse cultures in your classroom is necessary to success in teaching, in the 90's. Finally, it will be necessary in the 90's that college teachers continue to develop and improve strategies and techniques for the delivery of learning in the classroom.

Some characteristics of good teachers are:

1. They are knowledgeable, organized, and in control.

2. They are good communicators.

3. They exhibit a good attitude, have empathy, and are honest.

4. They appear professional and businesslike.

5. They utilize questions and other techniques to stimulate discussion and involve students.

6. They have a pleasant personality.

7. They are in control of various teaching techniques and strategies.

The First Class

As you approach your first class, considerable anxiety and nervousness will be experienced. This has always been true of teaching and will continue to be true in the future. In fact, many experienced teachers feel they do their best work if they are slightly nervous and anxious. Excessive nervousness and anxiety, however, can be a distraction to the teaching-learning process and efforts should be made to minimize them.

In preparation for the first class, keep in mind that it is nearly impossible to prepare for all eventualities. The speed at which the class presentation will go usually cannot be anticipated. Many times student response is significantly greater or less than expected. *Having excessive material prepared for the first class, as well as all classes, is worth the extra effort in confidence gained.*

Another major factor in facing the first class is to know yourself as a teacher. Anyone mature enough to be teaching has some feeling of his/her own personal characteristics. Most of us are average in appearance; however, we usually have gone through life compensating for variations from the average. There is no more need to be self-conscious in front of a class than there is in any social situation. Minor compensations may be necessary. If one has a tendency toward casual or even sloppy appearance, appearing neat and professional will pay off. If one has an untrained or light voice, practice in expression may be well worth the time spent. Generally speaking, part of the student size-up will include the appearance and actions of the instructor. Being in control pays off in not only eliminating barriers to classroom communication, but in developing self-confidence in teaching.

Remember, students usually are not solely impressed by the knowledge and experience of the teacher; they are equally influenced by related factors. Some guidelines for the first class are as follows:

- Plan an activity that allows students to get involved

immediately. This may simply be an information gathering format.

- Initiate casual conversation between yourself and students and among the students prior to launching into the specific course.

- Make certain you are early, at least 20 minutes prior to the start of the class. If possible, greet your students.

- Define and present on an overhead your course objectives and goals.

- Identify course standards including time of outside work.

- Use an icebreaker, if possible — something that is related to your course but does not have a specific answer.

- Take care of housekeeping items, such as breaks, restroom locations.

- Use tips from experienced teachers cautiously; they are coming from a different perspective and are different individuals.

- Conduct a class — don't meet and dismiss. First impressions are lasting.

Some successful instructors begin their first class by asking students to write a short paragraph about themselves and their concerns. Often students are willing to discuss their anxieties, which may help stimulate discussion and understanding later.

Setting the Tone

Professional educators and teacher trainers agree that the greatest task in teaching is to motivate students to feel good about the course in which they are enrolled. Creating positive feelings about the course is an important goal of the instructor. In setting the tone of the classroom, faculty often overlook a very basic human trait. Often they assume the students are aware of the fact that the teacher intends to be pleasant, cooperative, and helpful. This should not be taken for granted. With differing personalities and types of students in the classroom, faculty members must realize that a positive comment or gesture to one student may in fact be negative to another student. Thus, faculty should make a concerted effort to show pleasantness in their behavior. A smile, a pleasant comment, or a laugh with students who are attempting to be funny will pay great dividends.

It is also important to realize in setting the tone of the classroom that permissiveness is not always bad. We are all familiar with traditional teaching in which students were essentially "passive" learners. We are also familiar with situations where excessive permissiveness was a distraction to other students. Teachers of adults must be cognizant of the fact that flexibility and permissiveness are important to a proper learning atmosphere and that encouraging creativity and unexpected comments is part of the learning and teaching process. Excessive distraction, due to flexibility, can always be controlled by the faculty member who is the authority in the room. The instructor has ultimate authority and need not exercise it to prove it for its own sake. Remember, permissiveness and flexibility require considerable working skill. Authority is there with the role.

Teachers are Actors/Actresses

In reality, teachers are on stage; they are actors or actresses whether or not they recognize and admit it. A teacher in front of the classroom carries all of the responsibility and requires all of the talent of anyone on stage or taking part in a performance. Due to modern technology, unfortunately, students compare faculty to professionals they have seen in other roles. Thus, adjunct faculty must be alert to the ramifications.

Faculty members have within themselves all of the emotions

of stage performers with greater audience interaction. There may be, on occasion, an emotional reaction and one should prepare to deal with it. As an instructor, one will experience fear, joy, feelings of tentativeness, and feelings of extreme confidence and satisfaction. *Handle fear with good preparation;* confidence brought forward with good preparation is the easiest way to allay fear. Remove anxieties from the classroom by developing communication systems. Some adjunct faculty members are effective at using humor. As a general rule, however, humor should be used delicately. *Jokes are completely out.* Almost any joke that is told in the classroom will offend someone.

Classroom Communication

Many kinds of communication exist in every classroom situation. Faculty must be aware that facial expressions, eye contact with students, as well as student interaction are all forms of communication.

A major concern is that classroom communication be structured in a positive manner. Communication starts the moment the instructor steps into the classroom on the first day or evening of class. As is indicated elsewhere in this publication, the method by which the faculty member commences the first class and the initial interaction with students, is indicative of the type of communication that will exist throughout the course. The amount of student participation as the course progresses is an indicator of the direction in which the communication is flowing. Since many students today are adults, it provides greater opportunity to call upon a broader range of backgrounds. The discussion of facts, events, examples, analogies, and anecdotes will often elicit an association with your adult students. This then will encourage them to share experiences and anecdotes and comments of their own. Students with full-time work experiences and/or who have raised or are raising a family have varied and important experiences that they can communicate. The best communication device is still talking. Use every effort at your command to get students to talk. The use of open-ended questions will stimulate discussions. Class challenges in the form of problems and short oral reports should also be encouraged.

Gestures

Most non-verbal gestures are well-known to faculty and students. For example, eye contact, or lack of it, indicates many things. Casual eye contact will indicate disinterest or lack of attention or possibly even lack of understanding of the discussion. Extended eye contact may signal aggression or resentment on the part of a student. Effective and timely eye contact can reduce psychological differences between individuals and faculty. Remember, analysis of eye contact with the class can indicate if communication channels are open or closed.

Gestures or movements are other ways of non-verbal communication. Obviously, the ages old concept of pointing the finger by the teacher means "pay attention to the point." In addition to pointing, keep in mind that generally in our culture making a comment with the hand extended palm up is a positive and supportive gesture, whereas a downward direction of the palm indicates a negative reaction. Students are very conscious of gestures. Simply walking back and forth in front of a class, if it is not nervous pacing, indicates an interest in the environment in which one is working. Using the hands and arms to demonstrate space or extended distance is effective. Gestures can be instructional, supportive, and effective, or they can be distracting. Faculty should make every effort to determine which of the gestures are adding to the instructional process and which are personal mannerisms that may be distracting.

The Three R's

Much has been written about the three R's of learning. The author, however, feels that the three R's of teaching are equally important.

The three R's of good teaching are repeat, respond, and reinforce. Very simply they mean: student comments and contributions, if worthy of being recognized in class, are worthy of being repeated. A simple repeat, however, is not sufficient. One should elicit an additional response either from the class or the student making the original statement. After the response, reinforcement of the statement or conclusions should be stated. These three simple rules do many things to improve class relationships. They emphasize the importance of the student, students to each other, and what they say. They promote two way communication and represent applications of one of the basic tenants of learning — reinforcement.

Good Class/Bad Class Characteristics

To some degree the instructor will determine the personality of the class. Whether the class is a good or poor class is usually, but not always, influenced by the control, expertise, and strategies of the class leader/instructor. Below is a simplified listing that will help to identify the attitude of the class in general and to make corrections, if necessary, along the way.

Good Class:	Poor Class
dynamic	static
communicative	quiet
participative	tense
contributive	holds into self
active interchange.	does assignments only
	teacher dominated.

Teaching Styles

Just as students have styles of learning, it is appropriate that part-time faculty members recognize their own styles of teaching. In relation to students who view themselves as consumers, as well as learners and developing intellectuals, the style that the teacher brings to the classroom is relatively important. For example, an instructor who emphasizes facts in teaching will find difficulty in developing meaningful discussions with students who have progressed to the exploration stage of their learning process. It is not important that part-time instructors modify their behavior to match that of students. It is important, however, that part-time faculty recognize their own teaching styles and adapt teaching processes, techniques, and strategies to enhance their most effective style. Some questions in assisting in the self-determination of the teaching styles are:

1. Do I tend to be authoritative, directional, semi-directional, or laissez-faire in my classroom leadership?

2. Do I solicit communication with and between students easily or with difficulty?

3. Am I well-organized and well planned?

4. Am I meticulous in my appearance as a professional or do I have a tendency to put other priorities first and show up in class as is?

I have found that teaching styles, as many of life's other ventures, are not static. Many of the techniques used early in my career with younger students who appreciated humor and diversion were not as effective with later more mature students who felt they were there to learn, not to be entertained. I noticed in my later career that I had a tendency to be well-organized, have well stated objectives, use good class communication, observe all of the characteristics that I deemed important to good teaching, but I had become too serious. For that reason I now occasionally mix in with my lesson plan an additional sheet that says to me "smile, be friendly."

Also I found an evolution in the use of anecdotes. Strangely enough it was the reverse. Early in my career the use of anecdotes sometimes drew criticism from students as "too much story telling."

Later I began to put the question on my evaluation questionaires: "Were the anecdotes and stories meaningful?" The overwhelming response from adult students was "yes". They were meaningful, they brought meaning to the class, and they were valuable because the adults were interested to know of experiences from people who were actually practitioners. One note of caution, however; the use of anecdotes should relate to the topic being discussed and not simply be stories of other experiences.

Checklist for Part-time Faculty

There are many things that part-time faculty need to know when receiving their teaching assignment. Each teaching situation may call for new information. There are, however, basic items that part-time faculty will almost assuredly be asked at some time during class. This section lists several items that you may wish to check before entering the first class.

FACULTY CHECK LIST

1. What are the names of the department chairperson, dean, and director and other officials?

2. Have I completed all of my paperwork for official employment? (It's demoralizing when an expected paycheck doesn't arrive.)

3. Is there a pre-term faculty meeting? Date: _____ Time: _____

4. Is there a departmental course syllabus, course outline, or statement of goals and objectives available for the course?

5. Are there prepared departmental handouts?

6. Are there prepared departmental tests?

7. Where is and how do I get my copy of the text and supportive materials for teaching the class?

8. What instructional support aids are available?

9. Is there a department and/or college attendance or tardiness policy?

10. When are grades due? When do students receive grades?

11. Is there a college or departmental grading policy?

12. Where can I get instructional aid materials, films, video tapes, etc., and what is the lead time for ordering?

13. Is there a student evaluation of instruction in this course? Do I have a sample copy?

14. What is the library book check-out procedure?

15. What are the bookstore policies?

2

Planning

There are many suggestions for good teaching discussed in this publication, however, the most important activity for part-time faculty is planning. Planning is essential to a successful teaching situation. Many of the students in your class will come from a structured background or possibly employment situations where plans or even performance objectives are implemented. Over the past several years, planning has taken on added importance because of the legal implications for institutions concerning product advertisement. The best protection for this kind of action is to have a written viable plan.

Good planning involves a comprehensive approach, beginning with the course description through the student evaluation. Executing the plan is much like a football game; nearly everyone knows the standard plays and the standard procedures, but how well they are executed is what determines the winner.

Planning should take place prior to the first class. The preliminary steps should include familiarization with the textbook, organization of the material into content areas and topics, then ranking goals and objectives. An assignment of class time should be made to each of the major topics and a plan for a number of activities for each should be developed. In addition, some "fillers" should be developed so that they may be used for those class sessions when additional material is needed. Good planning includes several documents. They include (but not necessarily in this order):

1. The lesson plan.
2. The course outline.
3. The course syllabus.
4. Course objectives.

The Lesson Plan

The lesson plan is a must for all teachers. It should be used as a reference and guide for each class meeting. It should have a definite purpose indicating the main thoughts for each lesson. The lesson plan should be flexible to allow discussion of current events when it is appropriate. The lesson plan should be developed in such a way that if media or support activities are needed, a backup system is available in event the materials or equipment do not arrive or there is a mechanical or electrical defect. The plan should contain key questions and quotes from supplemental material not contained in the text. It should include definitions, comments on purposes of the class, student activities, and teacher activities.

Faculty should make every effort to make lesson plans reflect their creative endeavors and their unique ability as teachers. Often, the syllabus and to some extent the course outline are dictated to faculty. The demands for accountability and the goals of the institution restrict these two documents and limit their flexibility. Lesson plans, however, allow the greatest opportunity for flexibility and permit techniques and strategies unique to the instructor. Faculty may appropriately include personal experiences and anecdotes in the lesson plan. Shown in figures 1 and 2 are examples of a lesson plan and a sample form. *An effective method of planning a course is to construct at least one of these plans for each day the class meets, appropriately number them, place them in a loose leaf binder and maintain them as a record and a guide for activities.*

Figure 1

Sample Lesson Plan

Course # and Name: Algebra 101

Date _____

Session #9

Definitions:

1. Equation is a statement that two expressions are equal.
2. Expression is a mathematical statement.
3. Linear equation is equation of 1st order.

Class Objectives:

1. To demonstrate equations through use of various expressions of equality.
2. To prove equality of expressions through technique of substitution.

Student Activities:

1. Complete sample problems in class.
2. Demonstrate competence of sample by board work.

Instructor Activities:

1. Demonstrate validity of solutions of equations.
2. Assure student understanding by personal observations by seat and board work.

Major Impact:

Understanding of appreciation of solution of basic linear equations.

Assignment: Problems — Exercise 8, pp. 41-42.

Figure 2

Suggested Lesson Plan Format

Course number and name
(after first page simply number chronologically)

Date _____

Session # _____

Definitions to be covered _____

_____

Class Objective(s) _____

_____

Student Activities or Exercises _____

_____

Instructor activities _____

_____

Major impact or thought _____

_____

Assignment _____

_____

The Course Outline

While the lesson plan is a daily map for faculty to ensure their direction and activity for a given session, the course outline is much more comprehensive and allows faculty to monitor the map of the entire course.

The course outline is usually a formal document. The standard outline format will usually suffice to cover in detail the topics to be addressed. Generally, a topic need not be divided into more than three subtopics for a class outline. Detail more significant than three subtopics should be placed in the daily class lesson plan. *The purpose of the outline is very simple: to make certain that all major topics are recognized and addressed during the course.*

The two types of outlines most commonly used in teaching are the *chronological outline and the content outline.* Content outlines are used with topics to be covered in a specified content order. It is often called a topical outline. The chronological outline is self-descriptive. Courses which lend themselves to time and historic development lend themselves to a chronological outline. Even sequential courses, such as mathematics and science, where previous knowledge is necessary to function at a higher level, are considered chronological outlines. Content outlines allow considerable flexibility. They allow faculty to arrange the content of the course in a way that is most effective for presentation. For example, physical education faculty may allow students to actually perform an activity prior to teaching some of the basic fundamentals, so that the students can see a need for the techniques. Whereas a chronological outline would call for the presentation of the basic information, before an attempt to perform is undertaken. If one is teaching a course concerned with legislative, judicial, or community activities, it would not be necessary that field trips to legislative bodies, courtrooms, etc., be conducted in sequence with other activities in the course.

Although in most institutions there are course outlines

available, generally they will not be filed and maintained as formal documents. Often they are treated in the same manner as lesson plans, to be developed by the instructor. The formal document recognized at most institutions and approved by the college is the course syllabus. A sample of a course outline is shown in figure 3. Theoretically, a proper course outline is developed in direct relationship to the objectives written for the course. This assures direction and purpose of the outline.

Figure 3

Sample Course Outline

Statistics

I. INTRODUCTION
   A. Basic Statistics
      1. Purposes
   B. Data Gathering
      1. Samples
         a. Instruments
      2. Recorded Data
         a. Machine utilization

II. PRESENTING DATA
   A. Tables
      1. Summary Tables
         a. Table Elements
         b. Tables with averages
   B. Graphs
      1. Types of Graphs
         a. Bar
         b. Pie Chart
         c. Line graph
      2. Data Presentation with Graphs

C. Frequency Distributions
  1. Discrete and Continuous
  2. Class Intervals

III. DESCRIPTIONS AND COMPARISON of
  DISTRIBUTIONS
  A. Percentiles
    1. Computation of percentile
    2. Inter percentile range
    3. Percentile score
  B. Mean and Standard Deviations
    1. Computation of Mean
      a. From grouped data
      b. From arbitrary origin
    2. Variance formulas
  C. Frequency Distributions
    1. Measures of central tendency
    2. Symmetry & skewness
    3. Bimodal distributions

IV. PREDICTIVE OR ESTIMATIVE TECHNIQUES
  A. Regression
    1. Computation for regression formula
    2. Application of formula
      a. Graphic
      b. Assumptions of linearity
  B. Correlation
    1. Computation of Correlation Coefficient
      a. Reliability of measurement
  C. Circumstances affecting regression and analysis
    1. Errors of measurement
    2. Effect of range
    3. Interpretation of size

V. THE NORMAL CURVE AND STATISTICAL
   INFERENCE
   A. The Normal Distribution
      1. Mean
      2. Standard Deviation
      3. Characteristic
   B. Statistical Inference
      1. Employing samples
         a. Randomness
         b. Parameters
      2. Normal Distribution
         a. Standard Errors
         b. Unbiased Estimate
         c. Confidence interval
   C. Testing Hypothesis
      1. Definition of Statistical Hypothesis
      2. Test of Hypothesis
         a. Level of significance
         b. One-Sided Test
      3. Computing Power of Test

The Course Syllabus

A syllabus is defined in the dictionary as "a concise statement of the main points of a course of study or subject." Although this definition leaves room for interpretation (for example, what constitutes "concise"? and what constitutes "the main points"?), one thing is certain: The syllabus is the official document of the course. The syllabus is the document that should be shared with students and filed as a permanent contribution to the instructional archives of the college. Thus, it is probably the most important document in the educational process.

The reason there is confusion in academia concerning syllabi is that faculty members may interpret the definition differently. For example, a concise statement to one faculty member may simply mean the words "Chapter V", whereas to another faculty member it may mean enumerating the major points of Chapter V, describing each point and writing a complete sentence concerning each. Even though the syllabus is one of the most important documents in education, part-time faculty probably will encounter situations where such a document is not available. There are two reasons for this:

1. Course development and presentation have been left completely to the wishes of individual faculty members and they are not required to make it available to institutional sources.
2. Part-time faculty members may be teaching a new or recently revised course for which a syllabus has not been developed.

Development of the syllabus is a multi-step process. A good syllabus has several major parts. They are:

1. The complete name of the course, including the course number.
2. The name and title by which the faculty member wishes to be addressed.
3. The faculty member's office hours.
4. The text or texts and outside readings required.
5. The course requirements and grading standards.
6. The course objectives.
7. The assignments, projects, etc. to be completed by the students.
8. A complete listing of resources, outside readings, field trips, etc.

Objectives. The first major part of the syllabus is the listing of the course objectives. Listing the objectives for a course often is difficult for new faculty members. The tendency is to make certain that everything of importance in the course is included. This dilutes the purpose of the objectives and makes them less valuable to the teaching process. As a general rule, most courses can be adequately described by developing not more than ten to fourteen objectives. One must be certain, however, that the objectives are reachable, they are teachable, and student learning activities can be directed to each. This activity is covered in greater detail later in this chapter.

Student Activities. Following the course objectives, the syllabus describes the activities of the students that will result in their meeting the course requirements. This should include in some detail specific activities such as outside reading, laboratory activities, projects, assignments, etc. It is best to describe these activities in a way that they relate directly to the objectives. Significant attention should be given to the reasons for the activities and how they relate to the course. This approach conveys to the students the impression that the class is all business and that there is a purpose for everything.

Course Requirements. Next the syllabus should include a detailed description of course requirements as well as student requirements. This is one of the most important parts of the syllabus because it defines for students exactly what is expected. It eliminates the possibility that at a later date students will claim ignorance of what was expected. In fact, it is useful in this section of the syllabus to list the class meetings by day and date, the specific reading and homework assignments expected, and other activities and class topics to be addressed. Many experienced faculty members have felt that all this detail was not necessary until they found themselves in an indefensible position concerning student accusations that the course content was not adequately covered. Sometimes this section of the syllabus is broken into two or more parts, however, the general rule is that excessive detail is better than too little detail.

Resources and References. Finally, the syllabus should include a complete listing of resources, outside readings, bibliographies, visitations, etc., to which the student may wish to refer. Without fail, required outside readings and library reserve assignments should be specified. Again, excessive detail is of value. One need not be concerned if the syllabus eventually grows into a document of five pages or more. The students will be appreciative of the faculty member's efforts and the instructor will be adequately protected in the event evidence of course content or teacher preparation is needed.

The syllabus should be distributed to students the first day of class. Time should be taken to discuss the syllabus and details therein. In fact, it is good practice to go over the syllabus the second meeting of the class with description in detail of the activities expected of students as they relate to certain assignments and objectives. A good syllabus requires considerable work initially but minimal time in subsequent updates. Work put into the development of the syllabus will pay dividends. A syllabus is a scientific document and a work of art and it should be shown that respect in its development and use. Figure 4 is a sample of a completed syllabus.:

Figure 4

Achievement University

Syllabus

Name of Course:

      History 200

Faculty Name:

      Dr. Madeline Jones — Dr. Jones

Office Hours:

      MWF 8:00-9:00 a.m. 2:00-3:00 p.m.

      TR 1:00-2:00 p.m.

Text:

      (Author, Name, Edition, Publisher)

Course Requirements:

      Outside readings (general and reserved list), projects, etc.

Grading:

      Midterm — essay, 30% of final grade

      Final — multiple choice, 30% of final grade

      Class project and class participation (including quizzes) 40% of final grade.

Class Objectives:

1. To enumerate the events, attitudes, economic changes, innovations that lead to economic growth during ante-bellum era.

2. To describe the effect on social, political, philosophic life, and the nation's economic structure due to the growth and development during the ante-bellum era.

3. To compare the meaning of Jacksonian democracy of the different social economic groups in the American society.

4. To enumerate the factors that lead to Andrew Jackson being viewed as a popular hero and tyrannical President and an agent of special interest groups.

5. To describe the impact of political groups on Jacksonian democracy.

6. To enumerate the moral and social causes, other than abolitionism in ante-bellum America.

7. To describe the European influence on American culture in terms of economic expansion, frontier experience, and political and social reform during the ante-bellum era.

8. To describe the roots including economic, political, social, demographic, and diplomatic factors that led to American expansionism in the 1840's.

9. To describe the many different economic, ideological, political, and social factors that led to the Civil War.

Student Exercises:

Completion of all examinations, quizzes, and projects listed under requirements. The completion of the reading of texts, specific assignments by class session listed, and outside readings as assigned. Submission of an eight page topic paper (date) selected from a list of topics distributed.

Resource Reading:

(Listing of text, outside readings, reserved materials, special reference materials, and personal resources outside the classroom).

Writing Objectives

The development of appropriate course objectives has become commonplace throughout the 80's and into the 90's. No longer is there dialogue whether or not college courses will have objectives; it is assumed that all courses and classes will have objectives. Often the success of faculty members depends to a great extent upon their ability to develop and implement appropriate objectives. A brief flowchart shown below capsulizes the major components of the teaching/planning process.

| GOALS |—| OBJECTIVES |—| CLASS STRATEGIES |

The most important activity in this process is that of developing appropriate course objectives.

Fortunately, the development of good course objectives is not as complex and difficult as we previously were led to believe. There does exist, however, two remaining pitfalls. They are the tendency to write too many objectives that cannot conceivably be covered in the class and the tendency to write objectives that are clear to the faculty member, but may not be to the student. In this section we will present two very simple techniques to overcome those problems.

First, in order to avoid writing objectives in a haphazard manner, simply develop the course goals and write the objectives to the goals rather than to the course. Course goals are easily identified. They are taken from the catalog course description. Once the goals are identified and written, all objectives are written supporting the goal without the necessity of considering all the ramifications of writing low priority objectives. A simple format to use for this is to take a blank sheet of paper and put one goal on each sheet of paper. Then construct the objectives that will be implemented for each goal.

The second part of the process, clarity of understanding, can most easily be addressed by clearly identifying the descriptors to be used in writing the objectives. The descriptors used are few in number but concise in stature. Developing appropriate objectives is merely verbalizing and then writing down your thoughts concerning the objective you wish to develop. After the statement has been verbalized, apply the appropriate descriptors. They are:

write	solve
contrast	compare
compose	describe
recite	construct
compute	identify
list	attend

When writing objectives it is important that you can measure whether the objective has been reached.

Conversely descriptors that should not be used since they cannot be clearly measured for completion include:

understand
enjoy
appreciate
believe
grasp

It is not necessary to have conditional lead-ins such as "at the completion of . . .", that is understood. Some conditions may be included, for example, the achievement of a certain rating score or the achievement of a certain activity in a given amount of time. Make every effort, however, to be clear in terms of student understanding of the conditions. Good objectives are essential to a good planning process. You should be evaluating and assigning grades essentially on the basis of the completion of the course objectives that you establish. Robert Mager, one of the pioneers of the instructional objective movement, outlines several principles to be observed in writing objectives (Mager, 1962). They are: a. be explicit, b. communicate, c. tell what the learner will be doing, d. indicate conditions if there are any, e. include some recognition of it being achieved.

Examples of some well written objectives are:

1. The student will recite the Gettysburg Address.

2. The student will identify the major components of a successful lesson plan.

3. The student will describe the process involved in a bank approval of a consumer loan.

4. The student will write a five page news release on a selected, identified topic with a minimum of two errors.

Faculty Self-Evaluation

Many colleges today have forms available for faculty who wish to conduct self-evaluations. If used, whether voluntary or mandatory, it must be kept in mind that most of these forms are in fact student opinionnaires and not statistically valid instruments.

This does not, however, decrease the value of faculty seeking student input to improve their teaching. Whether you are an experienced faculty member or new to the profession, you will invariably find surprises while conducting such evaluations. New faculty members will be astonished at the quality of some observations students make. I recall an acquaintance who was considered by his associates and himself to possess an effective sense of humor. However, after conducting a self-evaluation in the classroom, he was surprised to find that the students not only rated him low, but many felt he did not possess a sense of humor. (Whether or not the results of student sampling of this type precipitate a change in behavior of the faculty member is not important). It is important, however, that faculty know how they are being perceived by the students.

There are two identifiable characteristics that are consistently valued by the students in relation to faculty behavior. They are:

1. Their business-like behavior in the classroom.

2. Being understanding and friendly.

Figure 5 is a form that faculty members may use to conduct self-evaluation. Note that the form exists in three sections:

- Classroom evaluation
- Course related factors
- Teacher personal evaluation

This form may be reproduced in its entirety if desired, however, there probably will be a preference, especially in sections two and three of the evaluation form, to add class-related questions.

The first section of the form (classroom evaluation) is an attempt to obtain insight concerning behavior in the classroom as it is viewed by the students. The second section of the evaluation form (course related factors) may vary considerably depending upon the type of course. Some courses lend themselves extensively to course related factors while other classes may not. The final section (teacher personal evaluation) gives the faculty member an opportunity to select some personal evaluation characteristics that they may wish to review occasionally. Questions may be added or deleted to this form at will.

Remember that student perceptions are very often motivated by personal biases rather than objective evaluation of the instructor. The continued use of a form of this type is helpful to faculty to determine if there are characteristics that continue to surface that need attention. Many statistical techniques can be applied to evaluation forms such as this. A simple method of utilizing the form is to ask the students to assign numbers 1-5 to each of the categories and then weight them on a number scale. It is not intended that this self-evaluation form contain content validity; however, it should be comprehensive enough to give faculty members insight into their teaching situation.

Figure 5

Faculty Evaluation Form

Class: _____

Date: _____

Instructions: Please grade each factor on a scale of 1-5 in terms of your perception of the teacher's behavior or characteristics.

Classroom Evaluation

Preparation for class   _____

Communication of classroom expectation to students   _____

Command of subject matter   _____

Professional and businesslike classroom behavior   _____

Tests and evaluation reflect classroom lecture,
   discussion and objectives   _____

Availability for consultation   _____

Encouragement of student participation   _____

Assignments clear and concise   _____

Course Related Factors

Appropriateness of project assignments   _____

Value of field trips   _____

Appropriate topic selection for outside assignments   _____

Utilization of supplemental teaching aids,
   support and other activities.   _____

Teacher Personal Evaluation

Consideration for differing opinions   _____

Consideration for individuals as persons   _____

Sense of humor   _____

Rating of instructor as compared to other
   college professors   _____

Personal appearance   _____

Consideration of students from different cultures   _____

Instructor's greatest strengths _____

Instructor's greatest weaknesses _____

Suggestions to improve course _____

3

Teaching Techniques and Instructional Aids

Chapter 3 is a discussion of some of the more common techniques and teaching aids used in classroom instruction. Although the utilization of these activities depends upon the style and personality of the instructor, the support described in this chapter is typical for most teaching situations. Instructors currently using some of these techniques may find suggestions for improvement or greater utilization in this chapter.

TEACHING TECHNIQUES

A variety of proven classroom strategies are utilized successfully by both full and part-time faculty. It is impossible, in a publication such as this, to go into detail for each of the techniques. Obviously, successful teaching depends to a certain degree upon the initiative, creativity, and the risk-taking ability of the faculty member. Some of the techniques more commonly used by successful teachers include:

lecture	discussion
question/answer	small group instruction
video	film
slides	field trips
visiting speaker	magazines and trade journals
self-prepared handouts	role playing
buzz groups	student panel
projects	student reports
term paper	outside assignment
chalkboard	overhead projection
newspaper	publications
lab assignments	computers
case studies	research project

The following pages describe the major classroom activities and provide suggestions for effective utilization.

The Lecture

Although the lecture has long been recognized as one of the more appropriate ways to convey information, there is often a fine line between instructors "telling" students and "presenting" lectures. Historically, the lecture was intended for highly motivated and well-informed listeners who were present to hear a specific topic discussed. It has been adapted in recent years to nearly all classroom situations and for that reason is not always as effective as it could be. An effective lecture can be used:

1. *For developing general interest in the main topic of the course.*

2. *For providing additional information on a topic that is being explored in detail by other teaching methods.*

3. *For presenting supplemental information that is not readily available in standard texts.*

The modern lecture involves the integration of technology and other activities into the total presentation. A good classroom lecture includes: coverage, information, explanation, and motivation.

Steps in building a better lecture include:

1. Build the lecture around major items or points.

2. Include activities as part of the lecture: audio-visual, guest speaker, etc.

3. Introduce the lecture by telling the students what the content will be.

4. Do not read, refer.

5. Over-prepare. It will enhance your confidence.

6. Use gestures. Remember, a hand or palm up is positive and down is negative.

7. Encourage students to interrupt.

8. Assist students in taking notes. Provide outline or allow time for note taking.

9. Document references verbally.

10. Prepare anecdotes and questions.

11. Don't depend upon memory, write it down.

12. Move around. Don't stand in one place or by the lectern.

13. Tell them what you are going to tell them; then tell them what you told them.

14. Refer to examples or other topics.

15. Summarize appropriately.

16. Tell them when you are starting, what your intentions are, and when you are changing topics.

Lecture Techniques. There are several methods by which you can improve your lectures. Adequate preparation with appropriate support of references, anecdotes, etc., will enhance the effectiveness of the lecture. Depending upon memory for such support may prove ineffective, therefore, references, etc., should be written as part of the lecture notes. Present a business-like physical appearance. Unkempt appearance will negate hours of diligent preparation. Cue the class to the major points to be stressed in the presentation. Provide an effective summary with repetition and reinforcement of important points. As indicated earlier, it is important that vocabulary and definitions be explained. It is not unusual to use the chalkboard or other visual techniques. It is also important that during the lecture appropriate time be allowed for student feedback, questions, and discussions.

Question/Answer

Questioning is an effective tool that may be used to stimulate classroom participation. Many experienced instructors make it an unwritten rule to call upon every student in the class sometime during each class session. The positive psychological value of involving students and treating them as if they were worthy of being asked questions cannot be overlooked. Questions are also motivational to many students. Pace the questions so that students have time to phrase their answer. There are several reasons why questions are a good technique for classroom discussion. They include:

1. *Stimulating thought.*

2. *Arousing curiosity.*

3. *Stimulating interest.*

4. *Developing student confidence in expressing themselves.*

5. *Determining student progress in the class.*

6. *Reinforcing previous points.*

7. *Evaluating the preparation of students.*

There is hardly a disadvantage associated with questioning if good judgment is exercised. Appropriate timing is important, as well as the type of questions and the vocabulary used. For example, it would be unkind to continue to question students who are obviously embarrassed and are having difficulty responding. Some students need to be "brought along" in the classroom.

There are several tips for questioning that are important. Use open-ended questions when possible. That is, do not use questions that can be given a yes/no answer. Use questions that elicit a comment or additional queries from students, even to the point of saying to an individual "What do you think of that, Joe?" Finally, questions should be part of the lesson plan and not a "wait to happen" item.

Questions have specific purposes: content, discussion, and stimulation. For example, a content question might be "What are the functions of a spreadsheet?" A discussion question might be "What are the advantages and disadvantages of a spreadsheet?" A stimulation question might be "How can spreadsheets enhance your job accuracy or a promotion?" This may be followed with "What do you think of that?" One would not normally pose questions as testing. This often intimidates students and negates the purpose of the question/answer process. Finally, questions should be addressed to individuals, when possible, preferably by name, rather than to the whole class. If your class is giving you the silent treatment, question/answer can bail you out.

Chalkboard Usage

Proper use of the chalkboard can be an effective addition to a successful classroom presentation. Too often teachers assume that chalkboard usage is relatively simple and/or they follow the techniques they learned from their teachers. There are two categories of chalkboard misuse that should be avoided: instructors who get involved in their work at the chalkboard and lose touch with the class; and instructors who are hesitant or fearful to do extensive chalkboard work for fear of losing contact with the class.

The chalkboard can be an effective motivating device, as well as a learning aid, if used properly. Here are some of the basic principles for using the chalkboard:

1. It should be used immediately when the class starts. Just the simple writing of the faculty member's name is effective utilization of the chalkboard.

2. The chalkboard, unlike a piece of paper, should be worked in segments from the right side to the left side of the room for right handed instructors and the opposite for left handed instructors. This allows the information the instructor is writing to be visible to the entire class.

3. The chalkboard is especially useful for listings, allowing the faculty member to write an item on the board, turn and face the class for discussion or questions, but not lose the momentum of the lecture.

4. Items that are to be remembered, such as definitions, should be written on the chalkboard. This allows the students time to write and allows the instructor time to pause and look over the class, encouraging comments, etc.

5. Steps in performing operations or listing principles and objectives may be written on the chalkboard.

6. All student assignments, mini quizzes, and diagrams (not produced otherwise) may be placed on the chalkboard.

Faculty should make certain that all information is legible and should occasionally pause and walk to the back of the room to view the board as the students see it. Talking while writing on the chalkboard, although difficult, is an acceptable technique. Remember to use a loud voice, to turn occasionally, and not to write for extended periods of time. When material is written on the board in proper order, it can then be incorporated as part of the formal lecture.

Sending students to the "board" is another technique that is very often overlooked. Although this may seem elementary and out of place to many instructors, it is a valid activity.

The Demonstration

For classes that lend themselves to this technique, the demonstration is an effective way to teach skills because it involves two primary senses — seeing and hearing. Psychological researchers claim that nearly 90% of learning takes place with the involvement of these two senses. Demonstration has other advantages:

1. It is motivational.

2. It is an effective technique for varying activities in the classroom.

3. It attracts attention and can be presented to groups or to individuals.

4. It is effective for large group instruction.

The demonstration is probably under-used as a teaching tool in today's classrroom. To be successful, demonstration requires extensive preparation on the part of the instructor.

Although demonstration carries the risk that it will not be successful, this is a small risk as compared to the benefits gained if it is successful. Students normally will not be critical of teachers who are not successful while attempting to utilize complicated techniques. They are much more critical of boring repetitious classes. To adequately prepare, the instructor should simulate the demonstration prior to the class presentation. This allows the teacher to examine the problems, be alert to possible difficulties, and even to forewarn the students that some steps are particularly difficult. Through this simple warning, the students will support the instructor and assist in making the demonstration successful.

The most commonly overlooked errors in preparing and conducting a demonstration are inadequate materials, tools, etc. A checklist of all demonstration materials should be compiled prior to attempting the demonstration. Above all, students should be aware of the objectives of the demonstration.

The Panel

The panel is an effective activity to stimulate student involvement. However, it must be structured in such a way that specific objectives and assignments are defined prior to the presentation of the panel. Such activities include stating the issues to be presented and/or defended by each member of the panel. After the presentation, discussion groups should be formed for the students to define their position concerning the topic. Helping students to develop open-ended questions to present for the rest of the class is an effective activity. A carefully prepared panel is a valuable tool for the participants as well as the class.

The Project

The project is an effective instrument that will provide students the opportunity and the experience of learning outside the classroom. A properly developed project will give students a variety of related activities from which to choose within their own sphere of interest. After topics are selected, expectations of the students for completion of the project should be clarified. Finally, the project should weigh significantly in the final evaluation of the students.

The Guest Lecturer

The guest lecturer is an under-utilized technique in most learning institutions. Most communities are rich with individuals who are willing, usually at no fee, to attend classes and to share their experience and expertise. The rapidly changing world in which we live makes it nearly impossible for faculty members to remain up to date on all issues. Inviting individuals who are on the cutting edge of activity in business/industry and community is a very stimulating and informative activity for students as well as instructors. Again, it is necessary to structure such a visitation so that the students are aware of the objectives of the activity.

The Case Study

Case studies traditionally have been valued only in sociology or psychology courses. Actually, the case study may be applied to many different classes. Students may be given case studies of individuals or processes in finance, investing, historic contrast, geology, or nearly any class situation. In a good case study, however, the instructor should establish the scene, the objectives of the case, and the problem(s) to be encountered. Students may then be given time to read and research the project and write their case paper or make an oral presentation. This may lead to student discussion in order to reach a consensus or conclusion. Case studies are normally assigned to individual students and not to groups.

Buzz Groups

The buzz group is an in-class activity. The instructor sets the discussion topic or problem and allows students to form small groups (three to five students) within the class. The students are instructed to address a specific problem and to do a comparison and contrast. The solution should be presented immediately on a flipchart or prepared on an overhead transparency for the next class session. Occasionally the instructor may have a solution prepared and use it as a discussion of the differences between the student buzz groups and the instructor's conclusion. Buzz groups should not be confused with small group projects. Buzz groups should be employed as a short-term, quick conclusion within a five or ten minute class activity.

Field Trips

Field trips must be planned so that the entire session of the field trip is on location. The activities that the class will focus upon should be discussed prior to the trip. Keep the class in small groups, specify to the students what they are to observe, and at the conclusion of the visit, meet to discuss the major points of interest.

Role Playing

Role playing can only be effective through the structured environment of a presenter, someone who reacts to the presenter, and an observer. The same individuals may reverse roles during the role playing process. To prevent role playing from deteriorating into acting or conversation, make sure the role-playing scenario is well structured.

Outside Readings/Written Assignments

Outside readings and additional assignments can be enhanced by the part-time instructor in several ways. Since neither the instructor nor the student is on campus for extensive library use, certain outside readings and references may be included in the syllabus. The process can be simplified if the faculty member prepares handouts and provides reference numbers to help the students obtain materials. In this manner, the students can more effectively use their time actually getting the material, rather than spending time searching. Again, being specific in terms of the topic and the objective are necessary.

Discussion/Critical Thinking

Good classroom discussion promotes independent thinking, motivates students, and stimulates creativity. It increases communication and helps students become active in the learning process. Discussion may be stimulated by utilizing critical thinking questions such as: "What is wrong with that kind of thinking?" "How else might this have been done?" "What are the strengths and weaknesses of this process?" Make certain appropriate time is allowed for discussion to emerge. A good discussion uses positive reinforcement for students who participate. In a good discussion the students address each other, not the instructor. Most of all, know when to conclude and summarize the discussion. This may be accomplished with a warning, question, or request for a summary.

Small Group/Large Group Instruction

Although not a specific classroom technique, there are different processes to be utilized in the use of small group instruction as compared to large group instruction. Normally, there are advantages to small group instruction because an informal atmosphere is an asset to both the instructor and the students. Students have time to explore ideas without requiring a definite yes/no response and both instructor and student have time for instantaneous, spontaneous feedback concerning established goals. There are difficulties in small group organization, however. There can be too much incidental conversation which can make it difficult to have meaningful instruction. Also, some students may have a difficult time because they are more accustomed to having information presented to them in a structured format.

Large classes have a tendency to be more impersonal and are more difficult to teach, especially to highly dependent and poorly motivated students. Large classes require greater preparation of materials, with more handouts and visuals. Since there will be less interaction with students, additional time must be taken to prepare and present meaningful and interesting lectures. If possible, arranging a 20 minute discussion group before or after class might be effective in helping students who are having trouble in the large group setting.

Quality Control Circles

Quality circles is one of the most dynamic and interesting concepts that has evolved in the past decade. It is a management technique generally credited to the Japanese (Weimer, 106). This technique can be very effective for instructors of adult students. It requires the involvement of employees (students) in some decision making activities of the class; is especially helpful for part-time teachers who don't have day to day contact with students; and is a relatively simple process. During the first class session, the faculty member requests 5 or 6 volunteers to join the quality circle. The group meets periodically, possibly during the coffee break or after class, to provide feedback to the instructor concerning the progress of the class. The feedback might include comments concerning: lecture, discussion, homework, testing, or other class activities. This process provides an ongoing feedback mechanism that includes the involvement of students. It may also provide support as the instructor implements the circles' suggestions during the class presentation.

INSTRUCTIONAL AIDS

Modern technological advances have made it possible for faculty to incorporate instructional aids in nearly any classroom situation. Gone are the days when one wheeled a large film projector into the room, made special arrangements for a screen, and called a projectionist to thread the film in order to show a simple 5-8 minute film. Although planning still requires scheduling, ordering, and the usual activities, it is far less complex than in the past. This section presents a brief description of some of the more commonly used teaching aids.

Overhead Transparencies

The overhead projector has become one of the most popular support tools in education. It is unique in that it allows instructors to face the class while showing images on the screen using normal room lighting. Overhead projectors are inexpensive and are usually readily available. Overhead transparencies of notebook size can be easily prepared and retained and are practically indestructible. Some projectors are equipped with a roll that provides a continuous writing surface. This enables the retention of information on the roll in the event students later wish to discuss specific points. This is especially useful in mathematics, engineering, etc.

Overhead transparencies can be prepared by hand at very little cost and printed on most modern copiers. They may also be prepared professionally to provide multi-color or other desired features.

Advantages. Overhead transparencies have several advantages over other types of media aids.

1. The equipment is inexpensive and usually every department has one or more of the projectors available for use.

2. The equipment is easy to use, requiring simply that it be plugged into a wall socket and focused. Sometimes the most difficult operation on an overhead projector is finding the on/off switch. In modern overheads, it is usually a bar across the front or hidden along the side to the rear of the base.

3. Overhead transparencies are stimulating for the class because they utilize both audio and visual activities.

4. There is no limit to the artistic excellence that can be produced on a transparency. Many faculty members easily prepare their own transparencies. Transparencies may be typewritten, handwritten, or drawn on standard size plain white paper, and instantaneously produced on a standard copier. Many times it is worth the extra effort to make a professional looking overhead transparency.

They are easily maintained, durable, and thus can be a permanent part of future presentations.

5. The use of overhead transparencies adds a professional touch to teaching situations.

6. They can be used in normal classroom conditions. No special lighting is needed and if a screen is not available they can be shown on a wall.

Faculty members who have not utilized overhead transparencies in their classroom presentations should write themselves an objective to develop some for their next teaching assignment. It is one of the few instructional aids that seems to have several advantages and few notable disadvantages.

Photo Slides

The modern technology of photography has allowed instructors to utilize the slide projector as an effective addition to classroom presentation. Thirty-five millimeter slides are a common instructional aid that are available at nearly all colleges and universities. They have several advantages:

1. They can be produced at minimal cost.

2. They are easily stored and used.

3. They can show many things that cannot be brought to the classroom or shown to students in other ways.

4. They provide a welcome change of pace to any classroom, have a distinct advantage over motion pictures in that they can be stopped for any period of time for discussion, are attractive, and usually add an aura of professionalism to the class.

The extra time it takes to prepare and maintain a slide carousel is worth it, especially to faculty who may repeat teaching a course. Many colleges and universities have established slide catalogues for their courses. Instructors should check departmental resources for this support.

Films

Due to the common knowledge of films, only a brief comment will be made at this time. The advantages of utilizing movie films outweighs the disadvantages. Most colleges and universities have their own film library or at least a catalogue from which films can be ordered through a processing service or directly from an agency. Faculty members should plan utilization of the films prior to the class and allow adequate time for obtaining the material.

Video Tape

Probably the most exciting instructional aid to come along since the introduction of the overhead projector is the video tape and the playback capability it provides. Video tape is an excellent and versatile instructional aid. There are several advantages.

1. They are easy to operate after minimal instruction.
2. Vido tapes can be purchased for nearly any discipline; films may be converted to video tape, and new subjects and topics may be developed.
3. Video tapes are relatively simple to modify in terms of updating content.
4. The length and duration of the video may be conveniently adjusted and may be stopped or reversed to emphasize points.
5. They are inexpensive.

Video tapes provide all the advantages of movie film, but none of the disadvantages. With the development of modern consumer technology it is possible for faculty to make their own high quality video tapes.

Flipchart

A commonly used instructional aid for business seminars is a simple flipchart. Most educators do not realize it has many advantages over the chalkboard or the overhead projector. The flipchart, a large tablet with pages that can be turned, is especially useful in allowing students in small groups or buzz sessions to record their discussions as well as their conclusions. It can also be utilized by the instructor and students for recording major points of discussion and descriptive lists. This information can then be retained by tearing off the page and taping it to the wall for future reference. A flipchart and a felt tip pen can be very effective tools in adding to the active classroom.

Handouts

Although occasionally overused in the past, handouts are still a valuable instrument for instructors. Modern copy technology allows for ease of preparation and update. Handouts should be used for material that students will need for reference, such as important definitions or computations, or position statements that may be discussed and contrasted. Handouts for lecture purposes should contain only an outline of the material discussed with space for students to add their own comments. A serious note of caution: *be careful of copyright violations!*

Innovation

In order to keep teaching stimulating and interesting, it is a good idea to try a new creative or unique learning activity occasionally. This may be something that is borrowed from another instructor or something self-initiated. However, there should be a plan for such activity. First, you might tell the students that you are going to do the activity for the first time. Rehearse it, try it on a colleague or one or two students to identify possible problems. Have a backup plan ready, but most of all, don't be afraid to take the risk. Share it with your class and they will be pleased that you are a risk taker.

4

Teaching Adult Students

Although it is difficult for faculty members to adequately plan in a standard way for all classes (because each class has a unique personality), there are fundamental activities that can be utilized in teaching adult students. One must keep in mind, however, that strategies and techniques for teaching may change due to changing technology and other cultural pressures. Therefore, they require constant reassessment and updating throughout one's teaching career. Techniques which may have worked for past classes or past years may not be the appropriate techniques for classes of the 90's. This chapter is intended to provide a better understanding of today's students so that you can make an appropriate assessment of your classroom skills.

STUDENT CHARACTERISTICS

The students of the 90's, whether they are older adults or college age, possess some common traits that affect classroom attitudes. These attitudes are often based upon the concept that students view themselves as consumers of a product, rather than seekers of knowledge. As indicated earlier, they will expect well-planned and prepared course goals and objectives. Other characteristics to be recognized include:

1. Today's students are more self-directed than their earlier counterparts. In other words, they generally know what they want and where they are going.

2. Today's students are highly demanding as consumers. They feel that they are paying for their education and are entitled to a product. There have been legal cases in which colleges have been questioned in this area.

3. Today's students often come to the classroom with rich life and educational experiences. They have read broadly and often have had interesting employment and travel experiences and may wish to share them.

4. Today's students expect to be treated as adults. They want to be treated on an equal basis and not as students or kids.

5. Today's students will demand relevance and immediate application. Relevance of the 90's, unlike the 1960's, is relevance toward achieving a goal or a career rather than social change.

Although the students are more demanding, they are also more interesting, more challenging, and will contribute to a happy, optimistic learning experience if given the appropriate opportunity.

Most students, being adults, are not in the classroom to compete. They are there to succeed and improve themselves. Teachers of adults should minimize the concept of competition and increase the concept of class cooperation and success. Above all, the age old process of x number of A's, x number of B's, and x number of C's, based upon a normal curve, has for all practical purposes been abandoned in the modern adult classroom.

Try to be considerate of the physical arrangement and comfort of the classroom when teaching adults. Adults will be easily irritated by over-heated or under-heated rooms, crowded conditions, desks that don't fit, poor lighting, inability to hear and see well, or other physical distractions. Although faculty members have limited control of these distractions, every effort should be made to recognize and allow for them. If physical change cannot be made, additional class breaks, standing breaks, and movement will assist the adult learner.

According to one author, there are six basic teaching functions for adults (Weddell, 29-30).

1. *Review of previously learned skills.*

2. *Presentation or demonstration utilizing previous knowledge that adults possess while at the same time presenting new knowledge.*

3. *Guided practice to develop mastery.*

4. *Corrected feedback to obtain corrected responses.*

5. *Independent work by students.*

6. *Frequent review.*

Student Learning Styles

Student learning styles are based upon the theory that there are differing methods for gathering, organizing, and evaluating information. Some people have consistent ways of selecting information and have dominant styles while others are more flexible in their approaches, depending upon the circumstances. Some people prefer to learn a skill by manipulating concrete objects, some by listening, some by reading a manual, and some by interacting with others. In brief, people have unique and characteristic ways of using their mind (Kazmiersky, 2).

Although the literature today contains numerous definitions of learning styles, for our purposes we will review one major system that is contemporary and relevant. The system to be discussed is defined by Bernice McCarthy. It is called the "4mat system." McCarthy states, after significant research, that by most standards there are at least four identifiable learning styles that lie on a continuum between concrete and abstract thinkers. The learner's style is revealed by the point on the scale at which the learner feels most comfortable. The four styles identified by McCarthy are these:

1. The imaginative learners. These learners perceive information concretely and process it reflectively. They are good listeners but also like to share ideas. They enjoy personal involvement, commitment, and are interested in personal growth. In class they expect the faculty member to produce authentic curricula, knowledge upon which to build, involvement and group work, and are willing to provide feedback. They care about fellow students and the instructor.

2. The analytic learners. Analytic learners perceive information abstractly and process it reflectively. They are interested in theory and what the experts think, need details and data, and are uncomfortable with subjectiveness. They expect the class to enhance their knowledge and they occasionally place factual knowledge over creativity. This implies that assignments and projects be developed to enhance sequential activities based upon comprehension.

3. The common sense learners. These learners perceive information abstractly and process it actively. They are the pragmatists in the class. They learn by testing theories and applying common sense, are problem solvers, and are skill oriented. In class they expect the instructor to teach the skills they need to be

economically independent in life. They may not be
flexible or good at teamwork situations.

4. The dynamic learners. Dynamic learners perceive
information concretely and process it actively. They
learn by trial and error and believe in self-discovery.
They like change and flexibility, are risk takers, and are
at ease with people. They examine reality and try to add
to it. They may occasionally be pushy and manipulative.
In class they like assignments to do on their own and
expect classes and curricula to be geared to their needs.
They seek knowledge for the improvement of society and
expect opportunity for experimentation without being
penalized by grades. They respond to dynamic
instructors who are constantly trying new things
(McCarthy, 37-43).

It is important for teachers of adults to understand student
types. The fact that all of these types of learners may be present in
any given class requires the ability to use a variety of classroom
activities. Some experts feel that the classroom activities should be
presented on a continuum to address the differing learning styles.

I recall an early experience as a college adjunct faculty
member that relates to this topic. Having for years been seemingly
successful teaching classes by encouraging open communication
and maximizing student involvement, I experienced a class in
which an acquaintance was enrolled. This person simply would not
respond or take part in class discussion. Knowing this person to be
social and bright, I was not completely surprised that when all the
student criteria for grades were considered, the individual easily
earned an A, contrary to my belief that all students must participate
to learn! It was years later that I realized that the student process for
learning was not flawed, it was just different from the style that I, as
the instructor, had perceived necessary for students to learn.

It is important that you review closely the previous

paragraphs because within the description of the student types is an important factor. That is, just as students have learning styles, teachers have teaching styles. Thus, you might identify your own teaching style from the above description. It is important that you understand your teaching style and behaviors and modify or understand that style in order to accommodate all learners.

MOTIVATION

Students may be motivated for many reasons: individual improvement, intellectual curiosity, needed employment competencies, change of career or advancing career, employment requirement, or the completion of a degree or certificate requirements. Although these motivational reasons are broad and varied, faculty must possess the skills to motivate students with a variety of approaches.

After many years of teaching, I remember being faced with a class that simply would not participate. Admittedly it was a Friday night class; however, you might expect that in such a class, highly motivated students would be enrolled. They were, however, very tired students and many of them were enrolled merely to pick up additional credits. After teaching the class about three weeks and experiencing very little student response, on the spur of the moment during the third evening, I simply stated, "We must start communicating. I would like each of you at this time to turn to a person near you, introduce yourself and tell them that you are going to help them get through this course, no matter how difficult it is, that you will be there to help them whenever they become confused, and that the two of you (by helping each other) can be successful in this course." This seemingly simple technique, in this particular class, worked wonders. The students became acquainted with someone they hadn't known previously, and surprisingly in many cases, found someone who really could help them get through the course. For the remainder of the course, when it appeared that the class was experiencing difficulty, I needed simply to say "let's take a

few minutes and get together with our partner and help each other."
When chalkboard work was given, two students would voluntarily
go to the board together.

This is an example of trying a basic technique of motivation.
In this case it worked. It may not work every time, but it was not a
technique that I had in my repertoire prior to that time. So, in
introducing this topic, motivation of adult students, be reminded
that faculty must occasionally try creative motivational techniques
that are not found in the literature.

Maslow's Hierarchy

It is virtually impossible to incorporate all theories of
motivation for your students. It is appropriate, therefore, that we
find refuge in a time honored theory of learning called *Maslow's
Hierarchy of Needs*. Maslow's hierarchy states that the basic needs
of human beings fall into five categories: physiological needs,
safety, love and belonging, esteem, and self-actualization. Maslow's
hierarchy is defined as:

1. PHYSIOLOGICAL needs — *feeling good physically
   with appropriate food and shelter.*

2. SAFETY — *the feeling of security in one's environment.*

3. LOVE AND BELONGING OR THE SOCIAL NEED —
   fulfilling the basic family and social role.

4. ESTEEM — *the status and respect of a positive self-
   image.*

5. SELF-ACTUALIZATION — *growth of the individual.*

Physiological, Safety, Love and Belonging. The fact
that Maslow's needs are hierarchical is a major problem for teachers
of adults. Attempting to address the needs of esteem and self-
actualization in the classroom, when physiological, safety, and love
and belonging needs have not been met, is a monumental task. In
fact, the lack of fulfillment of the basic needs may interfere with the

learning process itself. This interference may manifest itself in anti-social behavior. The characteristics of this behavior may include the following:

- Apparent lack of interest on the part of the student including general lack of student response
- A lack of communication with the instructor and other students
- Aggressive behavior
- Attempted verbal domination of the class or the opposite — withdrawal from class participation
- Constant complaints about the instructor and the college
- Absence
- Tardiness
- Complaints about the class in general

The challenge becomes, how does one in a short period of time, teaching on a part-time basis to part-time students, overcome all of these barriers? The fact is that one may not overcome all of these barriers. If instructors attempt to take the time to analyze each of the unmet needs of each of their students, they will have little time to work toward the goals and objectives of the course. There is, however, an important factor to support the instructor. It is that the need to achieve appears to be a basic need in human beings. The need to achieve, an intrinsic motivator that usually overcomes most of the other distractions to learning, is the factor upon which successful teachers capitalize. There is little faculty can do to help students to meet their physiological, safety, and love and belonging needs. The need for *esteem* and *self-actualization,* which are essentially achievement, are areas in which teaching strategies can be implemented.

Esteem. Esteem is the status and respect with which human beings are regarded by their peers. Thus, activities faculty members incorporate that assist students in building status and self-respect will support fulfillment of the esteem need. This is accomplished by providing an environment in which students can experience success in their learning endeavors. *Many learning theorists claim that success in itself is the solution to motivation and learning.*

One of the great fallacies in teaching is often stated by students who have succeeded in classes where other students have dropped out. That is the observation, "That prof was tough, but he/she was really good." This may or may not be true. The fact is that being tough has absolutely no relationship to being good. Too often the reverse of this statement is generalized upon and some faculty emphasize toughness as a substitute for good teaching. There is no known evidence to suggest that "tough teachers" are better than teachers who are "not so tough." It is especially discouraging to marginal students who are working hard when the chances for success experiences are negated by the instructor's desire to be tough.

Building esteem through success experiences is accomplished in many ways. Following are some suggestions that can be incorporated into classroom instruction to assist students to experience success:

1. *Make certain that students are aware of your expectations.* Students should be provided with course objectives in written form that tell them what they are expected to accomplish.

2. *Inform students precisely what is expected of them.* This means not only the work or the knowledge necessary for them to complete the course content, but also the time commitment required.

3. *Give students non-verbal encouragement whenever possible.* There are many ways this can be accomplished. Eye contact with students can very often

elicit a positive response. Gestures are important. The hand pointing upward is positive, downward is negative. A smile, a nod of the head, just looking at students with the feeling that they are working in a pleasant environment is in itself effective non-verbal encouragement.

4. *Give students positive reinforcement at every opportunity.* Simple techniques such as quizzes for which grades are not taken, quizzes designed so most or all students will succeed, as well as quizzes as a supplementary part of grading and evaluation are effective positive reinforcement. Comments and notes written on hand-in papers, tests, and projects are effective ways to provide positive feedback. Of course, the ideal form of positive reinforcement is provided through individual conferences and through informal conferences with students at chance meetings.

5. *Provide a structured situation in which the students feel comfortable.* The laissez-faire classroom is generally a lazy classroom. It is generally agreed that the structured setting with students participating in activities is much better than an unstructured approach.

6. *Provide opportunity for discussion of outside experiences by students.* Some students in your class, who may not be particularly adept at the course content, may have significant contributions and accomplishments to share in other areas. One of the greatest builders of esteem is to allow students to share their success experiences with others.

Self-Actualization. Self-actualization is the realization of individual growth. Such growth is realized through achievement and success. Self-actualization is the fifth and the highest of

Maslow's hierarchy. The suggestions below are some strategies that can assist in the student growth process.

1. *Each class should offer a challenge to each student.* Challenges are presented in a variety of ways. If they are insurmountable challenges they become barriers. Therefore, it is important that faculty plan activities that are challenges. Grades are challenges; however, grades must be achievable or they cause frustration. Course credit and obtaining the same is a challenge. Most students, even though they may not achieve the grade desired, will feel satisfied if they obtain the credit for which they are working. Assigning incompletes, allowing additional time for projects, etc. are techniques utilized to assist students in obtaining credit for their work. Questions in class, if properly phrased, can be appropriately challenging.

2. *Problem Solving.* The ultimate challenge in the classroom is problem solving. Problem solving techniques vary greatly depending upon the subject matter. Although it is impossible to discuss in detail here the ramifications of problem solving, this challenge does not lend itself solely to scientific and mathematics classes. It can also be utilized in many of the liberal arts-discussion courses through the use of professional journals, literature, outside projects, and group work.

3. *Treat students as individuals.* Individual conferences and the development of a system to allow students to get to know their instructors and other students are important. Many experienced faculty members do not hesitate to share with students their home or business phone number. Usually they are quite amazed how seldom students actually use it.

4. *Be cautious not to prejudge students.* Unfortunately,

stereotyping still exists in classrooms today. Faculty must make every effort not to "type" classes or students as "good" or "bad." Such stereotyping will affect grading and attitudes toward the students. Also, there is a good chance that the judgment may be incorrect. There is no place for stereotypes in education.

5. *Treat students as adults.* Many of today's students hold powerful positions in business and industry. It is difficult for them to regard the teacher as someone superior. To adult students the instructor is just someone in a different role.

6. *Give consideration to student's personal problems when possible.* Giving adult students personal consideration implies that attendance, paper deadlines, etc. may be flexible when faced with realities in the lives of adult students.

7. *Provide every opportunity for flexibility in the classroom.* Rigid rules concerning attendance, tardiness, test make-ups, etc. usually are demeaning to adults, usually are not successful, and may be illegal. The flexible instructor is the more effective teacher.

The previous paragraphs have discussed activities and techniques for the building of esteem and self-actualization of students. If instructors spend just 20% of their time on techniques related to the behaviors described here, the rewards will be exciting.

In summary, it is the belief of many educators that motivation is basically intrinsic. It is inside the beholder. It may be stimulated by external forces and must be cultivated by the student. Instructors cannot develop a set of procedures to guarantee motivation of students. Faculty can, however, be a "significant other" in the motivational process of students. The best way to motivate students is to be a motivated teacher.

TEACHING STRATEGIES

Although motivating students is probably the most important task that faculty encounter, being prepared with tried and proven strategies to assist student learning is an equally important function. Although strategies vary considerably among different teachers, there are some basic principles involved that are applicable to most situations. This section will discuss some of those principles.

1. *The instructor is a facilitator of learning.*

   Unlike the traditions of the past, faculty of today are not required to possess all of the knowledge available for a discipline or course. Successful teachers today find that their most effective role is that of a facilitator of learning. Knowing how to develop learning skills is more important to today's students than knowing all the answers. Over a period of time many of the answers change, but once students have mastered the techniques of learning there is no limit to their potential. Although this may appear to be a simple approach to teaching, it carries with it an additional responsibility — that faculty must become involved in learning as a profession, must read literature on learning, and must study the varied student types, learning styles, and other factors that affect student learning.

2. *Teaching effectiveness is situational.*

   It is a generally accepted axiom in teaching that no two classes are alike. Faculty must use all the historically proven teaching techniques (and some that are not proven) to reach all students. Students who are highly motivated to complete a program or achieve a high quality grade point average present different challenges from students who are struggling to learn. Each class develops its own personality. It is to the teacher's advantage to make it a happy personality.

3. *Understand the teaching situation.*

Many individuals reading this Handbook will have experienced the meaning of this statement. Instructors who have had a variety of assignments in different types of institutions will attest to the fact that there is a considerable difference in teaching situations. If you are teaching in an open-door community college or adult education program, you should be cognizant of the fact that students with a variety of backgrounds will be attending classes. Individuals teaching advanced classes in open-door colleges, classes with prerequisites, or classes in selective programs will find the characteristics of students very similar to that of institutions with higher admission standards. It is important that faculty assess these factors when preparing for their teaching assignments. Some questions that might be asked in making such a preparation are these: Is this class part of a competitive program? Are the goals clarified for both the institution and the student? Can student projects be developed so that the interest of students can be adequately explored? Is the size of the class a factor?

4. *Allow for individual differences.*

The diversity of adult learners today is significant. Differing cultures, as well as differing student types, will be found in today's classroom. You can allow for individual differences by giving individual help, knowing students' names, and being aware of students' backgrounds.

5. *Vary teaching activities.*

As indicated in the previous chapter, there are many

different activities that can be used in the classroom. Try new ideas. Some experts recommend that the teaching activity be changed every 20 minutes.

6. *Develop a supportive climate.*

Students must be made to feel that the instructor is there to support them in the learning process and is not a part of the elimination process. To students who come to class with a background of failure, this is very important. There are several things that faculty can do to develop a supportive climate. They include knowing the students by name, responding to them as individuals, being understanding and compassionate rather than authoritative, giving evidence of leading in learning, and involving the students in planning and goal setting to clarify expectations.

7. *Be sensitive to barriers.*

There are many barriers to student learning that must be recognized in order to be an effective teacher.

a. Unsuccessful previous educational experiences. Development of activities leading to early success will help to minimize the effects of previous failures. Being alert to early signs of failure and assisting students in techniques of note-taking, test taking, library procedures, etc. will provide support needed by such students.

b. The time barrier. Discuss time commitments with students at the beginning of the course. The barrier of time is an important one to working adult students and/or returning homemakers who have other responsibilities. Be fair and realistic. Don't use scare tactics in terms of the number of hours they will be required to study.

c. General procedures. Become knowledgeable of policies so that you can assist students with basic procedures. How are books checked out of the library; what about dropping and adding classes; where do they get a student ID or activity card; what are the procedures for taking part in student activities; buying books; where is the financial aid office, the counseling office? Knowing answers to these questions will help eliminate the frustrations of adult students.

d. Failure to understand their limitations and strengths. If weaknesses in reading, writing, or math skills are detected they should be discussed with the student in private conference. Knowing where students can obtain help or referral is important. Almost all institutions today have some type of remedial or refresher courses. The classroom instructor is the person who will first detect such deficiencies and be in the position to assist students.

e. Stress. As indicated elsewhere in this publication, students exhibiting irresponsible behavior may be reacting to deficiencies in the first three factors of Maslow's hierarchy: physiological, safety, love and belonging needs. Being careful to avoid confrontation and being considerate are important in stressful situations.

f. Physically handicapped students. Remember, many handicapped students do not wish to share their handicap publicly. At the beginning of the course it is a good technique to inform the class that anyone needing special seating, etc. to see you after class. Students can then take their new seats at the beginning of the second class (while there is still confusion) without undue attention.

Critical Thinking

Critical thinking can best be stimulated by raising questions and by offering challenges about a specific issue or statement. Many students still seek the "right answer" from the instructor. Faculty can assist students to rise above that level. Critical thinking questions are: What is the source of the information and how reliable is it? What are your personal experiences in relation to the information? What are other differing positions? What are the applications for the interpretation? What are your feelings on the topic? If students take a position on an issue, ask them for an alternative position. Be careful, however, to develop class rapport prior to involvement in critical thinking activities.

Feedback

As has been indicated in several sections of this publication, communication, student involvement, allowance for differing student styles and types, and teaching styles are important to the faculty member of the 90's. Equally important, however, is the ability to obtain feedback from the students.

As an instructor, you are aware of some types of feedback. However, it is easy to fall into the common practice for obtaining feedback: assessing student questions and answers in class. Listed below are several methods to gain feedback from students. Feedback from students of the nineties will be necessary for successful instruction. Feedback methods include:

class discussion
group discussion concerning
  a specific topic
board work
conference
body language
observation
graded paper comments
handouts
quizzes

verbal response
study guides
post-mortem
critique
ungraded assignments
ungraded practice
video tape
pre-test
utilization of "quality circles"

5

Testing and Grading

Testing and grading practices are of major importance to most students. It is important that we clearly define the purposes of tests and testing. Ideally, the testing process should be one in which successes are measured as part of a developmental process that informs both students and teachers of the progress made in the teaching-learning situation. Unfortunately, in practice testing is sometimes used for other purposes and anxieties are unnecessarily raised. These and many other related factors have a direct effect upon student behavior during the testing process.

Faculty must make every effort to prepare students for the testing in the course. This process starts by informing students at the beginning of the class of the testing procedure; when tests will be given and the criteria upon which they will be based. Too often students are heard to criticize instructors with the statement "they didn't test over what they talked about in class."

Ideally, tests are given for the following reasons:

1. To reveal to students their areas of strength.

2. To reveal to the instructor the student's progress.

3. To provide motivation for students.

4. To help instructors evaluate their teaching.

5. To provide a basis upon which grades are determined.

6. To evaluate students in terms of their professional and career goals.

Students and faculty commonly view the testing process as one for determination of grades only, when in fact there are more lasting and important reasons for testing.

Most experienced teachers are familiar with the major types of tests. The most commonly used tests are the multiple choice, the essay, and recall. There is less attention given to performance tests, oral tests, written tests, or short answer. For that reason the major emphasis in this description of testing will be placed upon the tests that are used most extensively. There are many types of tests: personality, aptitude, ability, career choice, diagnostic, etc., not normally used in the classroom that will not be discussed here. The major tests of concern to faculty members are achievement tests.

ACHIEVEMENT TESTS

Achievement tests are used to determine if students have achieved the objectives that the course intended. It is expected that achievement will reflect a measure of the growth that occurred in the student during the course. More specifically, it is hoped that such growth can be determined in terms of the cognitive, psychomotor, and affective domains.

Achievement tests are developed in many formats. The most basic achievement test, of course, is the written response. Most of the various tests known to faculty members, that is, multiple choice, essay, etc., depend upon achievement as their basis. This section will address primarily those tests. Before continuing with the discussion of tests, however, we will first discuss two important characteristics of good tests: validity and comprehensiveness.

Validity. The validity of a test is determined by answering the very simple question, "Are we testing what we should be testing?" In modern class planning which requires that each class have objectives, validity becomes less of a problem. *To maintain validity in the testing situation, faculty must be certain that their evaluation instrument and questions are based upon the objectives written for the course.*

Comprehensiveness. The comprehensiveness of a test is of importance for the evaluation of students. A test that is not comprehensive will not be objective or valid. To test students on a small sample of material taught during the course is unfair to students who may not completely grasp that segment of the course, but have understanding of the class in general. *Again, comprehensiveness is not a problem if objectives are written that cover a broad spectrum of the major purposes of the course and the test is developed for those objectives.* One must be careful to make certain that the test adequately samples the universe of the content which has been taught. The development of a broad body of questions covering the comprehensiveness of the course and then selecting from those questions at evaluation time can assure comprehensiveness without repetition of the same questions.

Essay Tests

Essay tests are one of the most popular tests. They are effective at any level of the hierarchy. That is, analysis and synthesis are easily incorporated into essay questions. Although essay tests require considerable time for students to respond, they do give an in-depth perspective in terms of overall student ability.

There are several factors to remember when writing test questions that require essay answers. First and foremost is the fact that essay questions should be related to the objectives written for the course. They should, if possible, be related to the objectives written at the analysis or synthesis level. Second, essay questions should incorporate a significant amount of content. Realizing that the students will take a long time to respond, questions should not be posed so that excessive time is spent on trivial matters. Finally, one must be certain that in terms of vocabulary, content, subject covered, etc., the student has sufficient background to respond adequately to the question being asked and that the question queried is not ambiguous or deceiving.

Essay questions, if constructed and graded properly, are the most accurate of the possible testing techniques. Although in recent years many teachers have resorted to some type of objective grading system, the essay question still provides the best opportunity for students of ability to express themselves beyond the minimum competencies required. Instructors who develop a high degree of skill in writing essay questions find that they can allow for flexibility.

Grading of essay questions presents the greatest difficulty. Keep in mind that essay questions are asking students to be objective, yet to generalize. The appropriate way to grade an essay response is to write the response from the faculty viewpoint and prioritize important items. Assignment of points to the prioritized items will then determine the grade.

The instructor must be cautious, however, that essay questions do not ask merely for student opinions. Theoretically, if one is asking an opinion, every student should get a perfect score.

Advantages of Essay Questions. The advantages of essay questions are enumerated below:

1. They provide in-depth coverage of material or content presented in the class.

2. They allow students maximum utilization of their capabilities in responding to an issue.

3. They are quick and simple to prepare.

4. They can be changed from class to class without greatly affecting the purpose of the question.

Disadvantages of Essay Questions. There are several disadvantages to essay questions:

1. They are restrictive in the breadth of the subject matter being measured.

2. They are time consuming for the students.

3. They have a tendency to weigh too heavily a specific part of the course at the expense of other parts.

4. They place the burden of handwriting, spelling, vocabulary, and grammar upon the student.

5. They have a tendency to lean toward subjectivity in evaluation.

6. They are difficult to grade.

Multiple Choice Tests

Multiple choice tests are probably the most widely used testing technique. With the implementation of computer scoring and computer assisted storage of questions, the development and maintenance of such tests are relatively simple. In addition, item analysis techniques, validity, objectivity, and comprehensiveness can be maintained with multiple choice tests.

Advantages of Multiple Choice. Multiple choice questions have several advantages that have led to their popularity. They are as follows:

1. They can be used to cover a broad range of content in a short period of time.

2. They measure the ability of students to recognize appropriate responses rather than to recall facts. (This is a significant benefit to older students who sometimes become confused with the recall of things they have learned.)

3. They are significantly more valid than true/false or

other related types of questions that have a 50% chance of being correct.

4. Students can be tested at the analysis and synthesis level.

5. They are easy to grade.

Disadvantages of Multiple Choice. There are some disadvantages to multiple choice questions that must be of concern to those preparing the tests. They are as follows:

1. There is a tendency to construct most responses for the knowledge level.

2. The questions are time consuming and difficult to develop.

3. They provide opportunity for guessing and elimination of responses.

4. They rely primarily upon recall and memory.

Preparing Multiple Choice Questions. The development of valid multiple choice questions is a significant challenge to the teacher. Listed below are several suggestions for the construction of multiple choice questions.

1. Compose multiple choice responses with four possible answers to minimize the guess factor.

2. Do not include impossible answers, they are easily eliminated.

3. Do not use such responses as "none of the above" or "all of the above."

4. Be consistent with the response format. That is, capitalization, punctuation, etc.

5. Do not use qualifiers such as "always" or general qualifiers such as "usually."

6. State all the questions in a positive format.

7. Keep all multiple choice statements approximately the same length.

Recall Tests

Recall items may be posed as simple questions, completion, or writing of brief responses. Although recall is involved in nearly any kind of evaluation system, specific recall of words that would ally straight memorization usually is not incorporated in adult student evaluation.

Advantages of Recall Tests. In event the instructor wishes to utilize recall questions there are some advantages. They include:

1. They are relatively simple to grade and construct.

2. Recall questions can address numerous areas in a broad field of content.

3. They require a specific recall rather than a guess such as may occur in true/false and multiple choice.

Disadvantages of Recall Tests. Some of the reasons that straight recall is not used include:

1. They may be time consuming to the student, that is, extensive time can be used attempting to recall something for which they have a mental block.

2. Subjectivity is introduced into the grading of similar responses.

3. It is nearly impossible to measure analysis or synthesis activities.

Suggestions for Development of Recall Questions. To utilize recall questions, there is some basic information that must be kept in mind. It includes:

1. Give information concerning the answer prior to the answer blank.

2. Clearly qualify the information so that students know

specifically the required response; eliminate generalizations.

3. Attempt to solicit responses at the analysis and synthesis level.

4. Pose the question in such a way that only one correct response can be given.

5. Allow sufficient and equal space for all responses so that the space does not tip off the response.

True/False Tests

Although they have their place in sampling of student responses or learning activity, true/false generally is not acceptable as being objective or valid. In event there is opportunity for its use, some suggestions are listed below.

Advantages of True/False. There are some advantages to true/false questions that must be considered for special circumstances. They include:

1. A large number and diversity of questions may be asked about a specific topic.

2. They are good to stimulate students and give lower ability students a chance at success.

3. They are simple to develop.

4. They are valid if only two possible answers exist.

5. They are non-threatening and familiar to students.

6. They are easily scored.

Disadvantages of True/False. The disadvantage and limitation of true/false questions are numerous:

1. Even with the allowance for correction factors, true/false questions encourage guessing.

2. It is difficult to construct brief, complete true/false statements.

3. Grading weight is equal for minor factors as well as significant points.

4. They are not appropriate for elaboration or discussion.

5. They tend to test the lowest level of knowledge with no consideration for analysis and synthesis.

6. They are typically low in validity and reliability due to the guess factor.

Constructing True/False Items. If one has elected to utilize true/false questions as part of their evaluation system, there are several factors to consider in the development of these questions. They are:

1. Avoid unclear statements with ambiguous words or trick questions.

2. Develop questions that require information beyond the knowledge or memorization level.

3. Avoid patterning answers with long strings of trues or falses or direct alteration.

4. Avoid direct quotes, as they will tip off responses.

5. Avoid specific descriptors or adjectives that might tip off responses.

GRADING

Basic Rules. Grading of students is probably the most difficult task for faculty. All of the elements of teaching: preparation, presentation, student activity, are reflected in the grading process. In addition, in an era of accountability, teachers are sometimes called upon to justify grades with documentation. Thus, the establishment of firm criteria for grading is necessary.

There are some general rules that are helpful in establishing the grading process. They are listed below.

1. **Communicate criteria.**
   Faculty should communicate the grading criteria usually at the first or second class session. A suggestive chart for this activity is shown in figure 6. Make an effort to allow students to respond to the grading plan in the process, before the first evaluation is given.

2. **Include criteria other than test scores.**
   Factors other than test scores should be included in the students' grades. This is especially true in social science courses where content criteria and problem solving are not easy to assess. For example, if it is important for students to communicate or express ideas, then class participation *should* be a part of the grading criteria. If a written paper or a project is part of the grade, students should be advised of the weight of the project applied to the grade. If laboratory demonstrations are part of the course, their value should be made known.

3. **Avoid irrelevant factors.**
   Avoid introducing irrelevant factors into the grading process. Including attendance and tardiness in the grading criteria is unwise. Many experienced teachers feel that if students possess the knowledge and show that they have reached the objectives of the course, they should be evaluated appropriately. This is especially true in teaching adults who may have significant career and business experience but may not have received official credit or course work.

4. **Weigh grading criteria carefully.**
   One should be careful not to overweigh certain segments of the grading criteria. For example, if one is to develop a grading plan such as shown in the diagram in figure 6, and then allow 90% of the grade to count for the final examination, they have probably defeated the purpose

of comprehensive grading. Equally important is the weighing of extra credit for extra work. If such a technique is used it should not penalize the students who do not feel it necessary to do extra work.

5. **Grade students on their achievement, not other students.**

   Grading should be based upon criteria of the course and not upon other students' scores. Bill Frye (Greive, *et al.*) best explains this in his discussion of grading. Several years ago, many teachers utilized a technique called grading on the curve. This technique essentially distributed all students in all classes on a normal curve and determined that 2.15% will get A's and F's, 13.59% will get B's and D's, and 68.26% will get C's. This system placed students in competition with each other. In recent years criterion based grading has found favor. Criterion based grading evaluates each student independent of other students based upon the criteria of the course. The criteria of the course are the objectives written for the course. Quite simply the students should be graded upon the degree to which they have completed the objectives of the course and not how other students achieved. Thus, if all students reach the objectives, they all should receive passing grades.

Evaluation Plan

In order to clearly define and delineate the criteria for assignment of grades, it is helpful if one first develop an evaluation plan. An evaluation plan is a very simple device usually developed in chart and worksheet form. The plan contains all of the factors that apply to the evaluation of the students. Across from these factors is listed the percentage that will be assigned to the various factors. A third column then indicates the points received for each factor. A sample plan is shown in figure 6.

Figure 6

Evaluation Chart

Grade Factors	Percent of Final Grade	Possible Points	Points Received
Tests	60	90	_____
Paper	20	30	_____
Project	10	15	_____
Class Participation	10	15	_____
Totals	100	150	_____

Note that any number of grade factors, weighted in relation to their importance, can be included in the *Evaluation Chart.*

The first step in developing the *Evaluation Chart* is to decide upon the *grade factors* and list them in the left hand column of the chart. Next the desired *percent of final grade* is listed in the appropriate column. This column should total 100%. In the third column, *possible points,* each grade factor is assigned the maximum correct number of points to match the percentage. This can be computed in two ways. The instructor may determine the total number of possible points that he/she will allow for the course, and simply multiply by the grade factor percentage (in example of figure 6, 90 points for tests is 60% of the total number of points for all factors — 150). In like manner, *paper* is assigned 30 possible points; *project* 15 points; etc. In the second method, the instructor may decide upon the number of points desired for one factor and work forward with a simple algebraic equation, i.e. (test factor — 90 points desired) 60% of x = 90; solution, x = 150.

The *points received* column is then used to record the points earned by the students in each of the *grade factors* categories. At the end of the term the *points received* total is divided by the *possible points* total to obtain the percentage used to determine the final grade.

Many modern computer grading programs (including the one

listed in the back of this publication) are written with formats designed for the use of *Evaluation Charts.* The programs then automatically perform the computations.

This system allows for flexibility in establishing documented criteria for the assignment of grades. It fulfills the need to have a viable grading plan and provides students with a process for their evaluation.

Item Analysis

A quick and semi-scientific method of checking the validity of exam questions is to utilize a technique called *item analysis.* Although appearing cumbersome and labor intensive at initial glance, item analysis is not a complex activity. One must keep in mind that item analysis will be applied only to those questions that need analysis or checks on their validity. Therefore, in most testing situations the process will be applied to only 5-10% of the questions. Item analysis allows one to check, on the basis of performance, the validity of questions, by determining if students who received the highest scores on the total test were successful in obtaining the correct answer to the questions being analyzed. Figure 7 shows a chart to use for item analysis.

Figure 7

Item Analysis Chart
Question No._____

Response	A	B	C	D	F
Correct					
Incorrect					

Item analysis is performed on one question at a time. Record in the appropriate blank the number of the question being analyzed. Next, record the number of students who responded correctly/incorrectly to the question in relation to their grade on the test (A-F). This process will clearly and quickly reveal the information desired; i.e., did students who achieved A's on the test respond correctly to the question being analyzed and vice versa? Thus, if there is no correlation or there is a reverse correlation in this comparison, it can be assumed that the question being analyzed is not a valid question.

Item analysis is a simple technique quickly conducted and greatly under-utilized. It is a very simple process to get an indication of the validity of questionable test items and provides the opportunity to reword or rephrase the questions so that they more accurately reflect the intent. As was indicated earlier the simple process described here is not intended to be statistically foolproof; however, it is certainly an improvement over the possibility of guessing concerning such validity, or worse, the possibility of leaving an invalid question or series of questions in an otherwise effective instrument.

SUMMARY

This chapter has attempted to review and provide some major criteria involved in the development of evaluation instruments, their validity, and their resultant evaluation of students. All of the topics here, of course, can be discussed in significant detail in entire publications. It is the intent of this chapter to provide adjunct faculty with structure in which to develop a valid and reliable evaluation system utilizing professional techniques and expertise.

REFERENCES

1. Bloom, B.S., *et al., Taxonomy of Educational Objectives,* New York: David McKay Co., 1956.
2. Greive, Donald, *et al., Teaching in College: A Resource for College Teachers,* Cleveland: Info-Tec, Inc., 1989.
3. Kazmierski, Paul R., "Learning Styles," *Teaching and Learning for Careers,* 1977, 2 (2), 1.
4. Mager, Robert F., *Preparing Instructional Objectives,* Belmont, Calif.: Fearon Publishers, 1962.
5. McCarthy, Bernice, *The 4MAT System,* Barrington, IL: Excel Inc., 1987.
6. Wendell, Robert, "Teaching Adults More Effectively," *Techniques,* 1989, 29.
7. Weimer, Maryellen, *Improving College Teaching,* San Francisco: Jossey-Bass, 1990.

Additional Instructional Support

Teaching In College
A Resource for College Teachers (Revised)

- Colleges — Curriculum & Clientele
- Teaching Strategies
- Motivation
- Adult Learner
- Planning
- Goals & Objectives
- Student Evaluation

200 pages approx.
$16.95 Softcover
$22.95 Hardcover

To Order
Info-Tec, Inc.
P.O. Box 40092
Cleveland, Ohio 44140
MC/VISA

Additional Instructional Support

The Magic Gradebook

Builds complete grading process from your Evaluation. Chart. Reports include following printed reports:

Evaluation Plan and Grade Point Scale
Final Grade
Summary Percent of Grade
Posting Sheet with Four Digit Social Security

IBM-IBM Compatible
384 K Ram
Fixed Disk
$89.95 (Quantity and Institutional Discounts)

When ordering please specify floppy disk size.
_____ 3½"　　　　_____ 5¼"

To Order
Info-Tec, Inc.
P.O. Box 40092
Cleveland, Ohio 44140
MC/VISA